TO EVELYN

EDITOR'S NOTE

The selecting, editing and publishing of the poems in this volume have been done without the author's assistance. The author himself is on active duty "somewhere in the Pacific."

E. K.

KARL JAY SHAPIRO

PERSON PLACE AND THING

REYNAL & HITCHCOCK

Grateful acknowledgment for the reprinting of many of these poems is made to *Partisan Review, Poetry Magazine, Common Sense, The Nation, Harper's,* New Directions: *Five Young American Poets,* and The Peter Pauper Press: *New Poems 1942.* To Dr. David Lovett gratitude is also expressed.

127130

811.5

S529p

PRINTED IN THE UNITED STATES OF AMERICA
BY THE CORNWALL PRESS, CORNWALL, N. Y.

CONTENTS

1

SCYROS   3
NECROPOLIS   5
THE DOME OF SUNDAY   6
PROPERTY   8
BUICK   10
TO A GUINEAPIG   12
EPITAPH FOR JOHN AND RICHARD   13
CONSTRUCTION   14
& CO.   15
OCTOBER 1   16
MY GRANDMOTHER   18
TRAVELOGUE FOR EXILES   19
LOVE POEM   20
DEATH OF EMMA GOLDMAN   22
CONSCRIPTION CAMP   24
THE TWINS   27
GIANTESS   28
BLINDMEN   29
ELEGY FOR TWO BANJOS   30
ISRAFEL   32

2

EMPORIUM   35
UNIVERSITY   36
WASHINGTON CATHEDRAL   38
ALEXANDRIA   40

THE SNOB 42

THE GLUTTON 43

HOSPITAL 44

MONGOLIAN IDIOT 46

WAITRESS 47

MIDNIGHT SHOW 48

HOLLYWOOD 50

AUTO WRECK 52

HONKYTONK 54

THE FLY 56

TERMINAL 58

DRUG STORE 60

3

THE CONTRABAND 63

NOSTALGIA 64

A CUT FLOWER 65

BARTER 66

SELF-HISTORY 67

PARADOX: THE BIRDS 68

HAIRCUT 69

HOW LONG AGO THE HOME 70

ELEGY WRITTEN ON A FRONTPORCH 71

TO EVELYN FOR CHRISTMAS 74

ODE FOR CLENCHED TEETH 75

DRUID HILL PARK 76

SIX RELIGIOUS LYRICS 80

A ROBBERY 84

POET 86

1

SCYROS

snuffle and sniff and handerchief

    THE doctor punched my vein
    The captain called me Cain
Upon my belly sat the sow of fear
    With coins on either eye
    The President came by
And whispered to the braid what none could hear

    High over where the storm
    Stood steadfast cruciform
The golden eagle sank in wounded wheels
    White Negroes laughing still
    Crept fiercely on Brazil
Turning the navies upward on their keels

    Now one by one the trees
    Stripped to their naked knees
To dance upon the heaps of shrunken dead
    The roof of England fell
    Great Paris tolled her bell
And China staunched her milk and wept for bread

    No island singly lay
    But lost its name that day
The Ainu dived across the plunging sands
    From dawn to dawn to dawn
    King George's birds came on
Strafing the tulips from his children's hands

    Thus in the classic sea
    Southeast from Thessaly

The dynamited mermen washed ashore
    And tritons dressed in steel
    Trolled heads with rod and reel
And dredged potatoes from the Aegean floor

    Hot is the sky and green
    Where Germans have been seen
The moon leaks metal on the Atlantic fields
    Pink boys in birthday shrouds
    Loop lightly through the clouds
Or coast the peaks of Finland on their shields

    That prophet year by year
    Lay still but could not hear
Where scholars tapped to find his new remains
    Gog and Magog ate pork
    In vertical New York
And war began next Wednesday on the Danes

NECROPOLIS

EVEN in death they prosper; even in the death
Where lust lies senseless and pride fallow
The mouldering owners of rents and labor
Prosper and improve the high hill.

For theirs is the stone whose name is deepest cut;
Theirs the facsimile temple, theirs
The iron acanthus and the hackneyed Latin,
The boxwood rows and all the birds.

And even in death the poor are thickly herded
In intimate congestion under streets and alleys.
Look at the standard sculpture, the cheap
Synonymous slabs, the machined crosses.

Yes, even in death the cities are unplanned.
The heirs govern from the old centers;
They will not remove. And the ludicrous angels,
Remains of the poor, will never fly
But only multiply in the green grass.

THE DOME OF SUNDAY

WITH focus sharp as Flemish-painted face
In film of varnish brightly fixed
And through a polished hand-lens deeply seen,
Sunday at noon through hyaline thin air
Sees down the street,
And in the camera of my eye depicts
Row-houses and row-lives:
Glass after glass, door after door the same,
Face after face the same, the same,
The brutal visibility the same;

As if one life emerging from one house
Would pause, a single image caught between
Two facing mirrors where vision multiplies
Beyond perspective,
A silent clatter in the high-speed eye
Spinning out photo-circulars of sight.

I see slip to the curb the long machines
Out of whose warm and windowed rooms pirouette
Shellacked with silk and light
The hard legs of our women.
Our women are one woman, dressed in black.
The carmine printed mouth
And cheeks as soft as muslin-glass belong
Outright to one dark dressy man,
Merely a swagger at her curvy side.

This is their visit to themselves:
All day from porch to porch they weave
A nonsense pattern through the even glare,

Stealing in surfaces
Cold vulgar glances at themselves.

And high up in the heated room all day
I wait behind the plate glass pane for one,
Hot as a voyeur for a glimpse of one,
The vision to blot out this woman's sheen;
All day my sight records expensively
Row-houses and row-lives.

But nothing happens; no diagonal
With melting shadow falls across the curb:
Neither the blinded negress lurching through fatigue,
Nor exiles bleeding from their pores,
Nor that bright bomb slipped lightly from its rack
To splinter every silvered glass and crystal prism,
Witch-bowl and perfume bottle
And billion candle-power dressing-bulb,
No direct hit to smash the shatter-proof
And lodge at last the quivering needle
Clean in the eye of one who stands transfixed
In fascination of her brightness.

PROPERTY

TO BUILD a bridge they cleaved clean as sweep of giant
    plow in loose loam
A mile of solid city,
Bursting to sun the once-sealed home
And baring the garden secret at the back,
Sending away forever the roomers and their meaningless
    children.

Like camera eye
But not pure of pity
I click click the shutter of sight,
Taking at odd angles the bitter scene,
The cornice cracked
The turned-over tree
And like wires down
Dangling ivy.

Devalued now for houses this property lacks all that
    reflected
A sweet slow century,
The ornate habits of another country,
The cast-iron lion and the mansard roof,
And of owners the self-quietus of ownership.

Built upon privilege this area was quietly honored;
Pride was its legacy and peace compounded
Till on heavy facades it hung hushed and heavy as death

Now nowhere are those tenants to be found
Who bestowed on later citizens their oldest sections,

8

But north of the city in their English valleys
Their sons and daughters
Continue the management of a large inheritance
Of joy and fashion.

BUICK

AS a sloop with a sweep of immaculate wing on her deli-
cate spine
And a keel as steel as a root that holds in the sea as she
leans,
Leaning and laughing, my warm-hearted beauty, you ride,
you ride,
You tack on the curves with parabola speed and a kiss of
goodbye,
Like a thoroughbred sloop, my new high-spirited spirit, my
kiss.

As my foot suggests that you leap in the air with your hips
of a girl,
My finger that praises your wheel and announces your
voices of song,
Flouncing your skirts, you blueness of joy, you flirt of po-
liteness,
You leap, you intelligence, essence of wheelness with silvery
nose,
And your platinum clocks of excitement stir like the hairs
of a fern.

But how alien you are from the booming belts of your birth
and the smoke
Where you turned on the stinging lathes of Detroit and
Lansing at night
And shrieked at the torch in your secret parts and the
amorous tests,

But now with your eyes that enter the future of roads you
    forget;
You are all instinct with your phosphorous glow and your
    streaking hair.

And now when we stop it is not as the bird from the shell
    that I leave
Or the leathery pilot who steps from his bird with a sneer
    of delight,
And not as the ignorant beast do you squat and watch me
    depart,
But with exquisite breathing you smile, with satisfaction of
    love,
And I touch you again as you tick in the silence and settle
    in sleep.

TO A GUINEAPIG

WHAT do you care, dear total stranger,
For the successful failure of my safest danger,
My pig in the poke or dog in the manger,

Or who does what in the where of his chamber
Probing for his gallstones and the rods of amber
When the succubae sing and the accusers clamber?

Tooth for a Tooth, O why will you wander
After somebody's anybody's body to squander?
Do the heads grow bald as the hands grow fonder?

Thank you. Your kiss of conditional surrender
Reminds me of the case of dubious gender
Who died on the verge of gaining a defender.

Then read it and weep, dear lovelorn panther;
Change your pajamas and fill the decanter;
Down with the dreamwork and long live the banter.

EPITAPH FOR JOHN AND RICHARD

THERE goes the clock; there goes the sun;
Greenwich is right with Arlington;
The signal's minutes are signifying
That somebody old has finished dying,
That somebody young has just begun.

What do you think you earned today
Except the waste, except the pay,
Except the power to be spending?
And now your year is striking, ending,
What do you think you have put away?

Only a promise, only a life
Squandered in secret with a wife
In bedtime feigning and unfeigning;
The blood has long since ceased complaining;
The clock has satisfied the strife.

They will not cast your honored head
Or say from lecterns what you said,
But only keep you with them all
Committed in the City Hall;
Once born, once married, and once dead.

CONSTRUCTION

THE confines of a city block
Cut to a monument, exact,
At all points rectilinear,
From air a perfect square intact,

As trim as Plato thought or Eu-
Clid drew with stick. What thinker put
This idea into cubes to sell
At fifty cents a cubic foot?

O neat, O dead, what feeling thing
Could buy so bare! O dead, O neat,
What beating heart could sink to buy
The copy of the die complete!

& CO.

WHEN he was twenty the nice whites of his eyes
Clouded to dense colloids and thickly sank
Into their sockets; once down town they froze,
Clicked in his head like dice and neatly shot
A loud typewriter and a roll-top desk.

"I look back on it now that was a school
For painting names upon the frosted glass,
Founding the children, thinking of a Ford,
Smiling at Sunday as at petty cash,
While bonds hatched secretly in olive safes."

The male is born with pulleys in his neck
That run up flags at daybreak for all ships;
See the white collars of the mind march on
To tilt the human angle of the nose
And shell the town with snorts and so debouch.

OCTOBER 1

THAT season when the leaf deserts the bole
And half-dead see-saws through the October air
Falling face-downward on the walks to print
The decalcomania of its little soul—
Hardly has the milkman's sleepy horse
On wooden shoes echoed across the blocks,
When with its back jaws open like a dredge
The van comes lumbering up the curb to someone's door
    and knocks.

And four black genii muscular and shy
Holding their shy caps enter the first room
Where someone hurriedly surrenders up
The thickset chair, the mirror half awry,
Then to their burdens stoop without a sound.
One with his bare hands rends apart the bed,
One stuffs the china-barrel with stale print,
To bear the sofa toward the door with dark funereal tread.

The corner lamp, the safety eye of night,
Enveloped in the sun blinks and goes blind
And soon the early risers pick their way
Through kitchenware and pillows bolt upright.
The bureau on the sidewalk with bare back
And wrinkling veneer is most disgraced,
The sketch of Paris suffers in the wind,
Only the bike, its nose against the wall, does not show haste

Two hours—the movers mop their neck and look
Filing through dust and echoes back and forth.

The halls are hollow and all the floors are cleared
Bare to the last board, to the most secret nook;
But on the street a small chaos survives
That slowly now the leviathan ingests,
And schoolboys and stenographers stare at
The truck, the house, the husband in his hat who stands and
    rests.

He turns with miserable expectant face
And for the last time enters. On the wall
A picture-stain spreads from the nail-hole down.
Each object live and dead has left its trace.
He leaves his key; but as he quickly goes
This question comes behind: Did someone die?
Is someone rich or poor, better or worse?
What shall uproot a house and bring this care into his eye?

MY GRANDMOTHER

MY GRANDMOTHER moves to my mind in context
    of sorrow
And, as if apprehensive of near death, in black;
Whether erect in chair, her dry and corded throat
    harangued by grief,
Or at ragged book bent in Hebrew prayer,
Or gentle, submissive, and in tears to strangers;
Whether in sunny parlor or back of drawn blinds.

Though time and tongue made any love disparate,
On daguerreotype with classic perspective
Beauty I sigh and soften at is hers.
I pity her life of deaths, the agony of her own,
But most that history moved her through
Stranger lands and many houses,
Taking her exile for granted, confusing
The tongues and tasks of her children's children.

TRAVELOGUE FOR EXILES

LOOK and remember. Look upon this sky;
Look deep and deep into the sea-clean air,
The unconfined, the terminus of prayer.
Speak now and speak into the hallowed dome.
What do you hear? What does the sky reply?
The heavens are taken: this is not your home.

Look and remember. Look upon this sea;
Look down and down into the tireless tide.
What of a life below, a life inside,
A tomb, a cradle in the curly foam?
The waves arise; sea-wind and sea agree
The waters are taken: this is not your home.

Look and remember. Look upon this land,
Far, far across the factories and the grass.
Surely, there, surely, they will let you pass.
Speak then and ask the forest and the loam.
What do you hear? What does the land command?
The earth is taken: this is not your home.

LOVE POEM

ATTEMPTED suicide was your tour de force
Against defeat, a promissory curse,
An act of nakedness, your first attempt,
The most vital, an earnest stroke of luck.

They screaming picked you off the kitchen floor,
Rushed at the gas range, at the windows, fumbled
The phone. It cut their throat and nostrils. It hurt,
The hoarse hard exhalation of the burners.

I was there when the doctor pocketed his watch
And stood up. I was one among the heads
Converged like cameras on your waking. For
Your giant eyes opened and you vomited.

Resentment died in convalescence; what
Had swelled you like a pregnancy lay dead;
And now gave existence to that same respect
Which to have mothered made you want to die

I heard one say, "Her gift was to be seen,
And poor. With sometimes spastic hate could foil
Her sister's husband and her mother's ulcer.
Called for in sealed and guarded cars could flee

Like wit across theatrical frontiers.
She was born among the mirrors of the bars
In the eyes of scions of important Jews
Whose gaze like marbles searched her dress, and paid.

Interpret it: the callous of the index
Kissed by the boss's son. The unreal wage
Of the big comptometer. The hours between
Punchclock, alarmclock. To the simple wish to sleep."

And you, "Life seeks its level, looking out;
Is physical, overt, uneasy lover.
Witness who put a high price on the money,
And, came for every whore, never forgave us."

Believe me, your intransigent good nature
Evokes, like inward joy of gas, a view
Of peace, a politics of strength, a pride
The touch germane to ecstasy requires.

DEATH OF EMMA GOLDMAN

TRIUMPHANT at the final breath,
    Their senile God, their cops,
All the authorities and friends pro tem
Passing her pillow, keeping her concerned.
But the cowardly obit was already written:
Morning would know she was a common slut.

    Russians who stood for tragedy
      Were sisters all around;
Dark conscience of the family, down she lay
To end the career of passion, brain a bruise;
And mother-wonder filled her like a tide,
Rabid and raging discipline to bear.

    In came the monarchist, a nurse,
      And covered up her eyes;
Volkstaat of hate took over: suddenly
The Ego gagged, the Conscious overpowered,
The Memory beaten to a pulp, she fell.
It remained to hide the body, or make it laugh.

    Yet not to sink her name in coin
      Like Caesar was her wish,
To come alive like Frick, conjecture maps,
Or speak with kings of low mentality,
But to be left alone, a law to scorn
Of all, and none more honored than the least.

    This way she died, though premature
      Her clarity for others;

For it was taught that, listening, the soul
Lost track and merged with trespasses and spies
Whose black renown shook money like a rat
And showed up grass a mortmain property.

CONSCRIPTION CAMP

YOUR landscape sickens with a dry disease
Even in May, Virginia, and your sweet pines
Like Frenchmen runted in a hundred wars
Are of a child's height in these battlefields.

For Wilson sowed his teeth where generals prayed
—High-sounding Lafayette and sick-eyed Lee—
The loud Elizabethan crashed your swamps
Like elephants and the subtle Indian fell.

Is it for love, you ancient-minded towns,
That on the tidy grass of your great graves
And on your roads and riverways serene
Between the corn with green flags in a row,

Wheat amorous as hair and hills like breasts
Each generation, ignorant of the last,
Mumbling in sheds, embarrassed to salute,
Comes back to choke on etiquette of hate?

You manufacture history like jute—
Labor is cheap, Virginia, for high deeds,
But in your British dream of reputation
The black man is your conscience and your cost.

Here on the plains perfect for civil war
The clapboard city like a weak mirage
Of order rises from the sand to house
These thousands and the paranoid Monroe;

The sunrise gun rasps in the throat of heaven;
The lungs of dawn are heavy and corrupt;

We hawk and spit; our flag walks through the air
Breathing hysteria thickly in each face.

Through the long school of day, absent in heart,
Distant in every thought but self we tread,
Wheeling in blocks like large expensive toys
That never understand except through fun.

To steal aside as aimlessly as curs
Is our desire; to stare at corporals
As sceptically as boys; not to believe
The misty-eyed letter and the cheap snap-shot.

To cross the unnatural frontier of your name
Is our free dream, Virginia, and beyond,
White and unpatriotic in our beds,
To rise from sleep like driftwood out of surf.

But stricter than parole is this same wall
And these green clothes, a secret on the fields,
In towns betray us to the arresting touch
Of lady-wardens, good and evil wives.

And far and fabulous is the word "Outside"
Like "Europe" when the midnight liners sailed,
Leaving a wake of ermine on the tide
Where rubies drowned and eyes were softly drunk.

Still we abhor your news and every voice
Except the Personal Enemy's, and songs
That pumped by the great central heart of love
On tides of energy at evening come.

Instinctively to break your compact law
Box within box, Virginia, and throw down
The dangerous bright habits of pure form
We struggle hideously and cry for fear.

25

And like a very tired whore who stands
Wrapped in the sensual crimson of her art
High in the tired doorway of a street
And beckons half-concealed the passerby,

The sun, Virginia, on your Western stairs
Pauses and smiles away between the trees,
Motioning the soldier overhill to town
To his determined hungry burst of joy.

THE TWINS

LIKENESS has made them animal and shy.
See how they turn their full gaze left and right,
Seeking the other, yet not moving close;
Nothing in their relationship is gross,
But soft, conspicuous, like giraffes. And why
Do they not speak except by sudden sight?

Sisters kiss freely and unsubtle friends
Wrestle like lovers; brothers loudly laugh:
These in a dreamier bondage dare not touch.
Each is the other's soul and hears too much
The heartbeat of the other; each apprehends
The sad duality and the imperfect half.

The one lay sick, the other wandered free,
But like a child to a small plot confined
Walked a short way and dumbly reappeared.
Is it not all-in-all of what they feared,
The single death, the obvious destiny
That maims the miracle their will designed?

For they go emptily from face to face,
Keeping the instinctive partnership of birth
A ponderous marriage and a sacred name;
Theirs is the pride of shouldering each the same
The old indignity of Esau's race
And Dromio's denouement of tragic mirth.

(March 21, 1942. At sea)

27

GIANTESS

WHEN Nature once in lustful hot undress
Conceived gargantuan offspring, then would I
Have loved to live near a young giantess,
Like a voluptuous cat at a queen's feet.

To see her body flower with her desire
And freely spread out in its dreadful play,
Guess if her heart concealed some heavy fire
Whose humid smokes would swim upon her eye.

To feel at leisure her stupendous shapes,
Crawl on the cliffs of her enormous knees,
And, when the unhealthy sun's fatigued

Have her stretch out across the plains and so
Sleep in the shadows of her breasts at ease
Like a small hamlet at a mountain's base.

(Baudelaire translation)

BLINDMEN

CONSIDER them, my soul, the frightful blind!
Like mannikins, ridiculous, unbowed,
Singular, terrible, like somnambulists,
Darting their eyeballs overcast with cloud.

Their eyes from which the holy light has fled
As if far off they see, always look up;
Upon the stones of streets never look down
Inclining wearily their weighted head. . . .

This way traverse the ever-enduring Dark,
Brother of Silence.—O Metropolis,
When all about you laugh and shout your song

With pleasure seized before this very wrong,
I cry, "I also drag myself behind!
What do they seek in Heaven, the truly blind?"

(Baudelaire translation)

29

ELEGY FOR TWO BANJOS

HAUL up the flag, you mourners,
　　Not half-mast but all the way;
The funeral is done and disbanded;
　　The devil's had the final say.

O Mistress and wife too pensive,
　　Pallbearers and priestly men,
Put your black clothes in the attic,
　　And get up on your feet again.

Death did his job like a scholar,
　　A most unusual case,
Death did his job like a gentleman;
　　He barely disturbed the face.

You packed him in a handsome carton,
　　Set the lid with silver screws;
You dug a dark pit in the graveyard
　　To tell the white worms the news.

Now you've nothing left to remember,
　　Nothing but the words he wrote,
But they'll never let you remember,
　　Only stick like a bone in your throat.

O if I'd been his wife or mistress,
　　His pallbearer or his parish priest,
I'd have kept him at home forever—
　　Or as long as bric-a-brac at least.

I would have burned his body
　　And salvaged a sizeable bone

For a paper-weight or a door-stop
    Or a garden flagstone.

I would have heaped the fire
    And boiled his beautiful skull.
It was laden like a ship for travels
    And now is but an empty hull.

I would have dried it off in linens,
    Polished it with a chamois cloth
Till it shone like a brand-new quarter
    And felt smooth as the nose of a moth.

Or I'd have hung it out in the garden
    Where everything else is alive,
Put a queen-bee in the brain case
    So the bees could build a hive.

Maybe I'd have wired the jawbone
    With a silver spring beneath,
Set it in the cradle with baby
    So baby could rattle the teeth.

O you didn't do right by William
    To shove him down that filthy hole,
Throw him a lot of tears and Latin
    And a cheap "God bless your soul."

You might as well leave off mourning,
    His photograph is getting dim,
So you'd better take a long look at it
    For it's all you'll ever see of him.

Haul up the flag you mourners,
    Not half-mast but all the way,
The funeral is done and disbanded,
    The devil's had the final say.

ISRAFEL

PICTURE the grave in his diabolical dream
Where death would come with clues and scenery,
The bulbous forehead and the crooked mouth
Leaking a poison, the translucent hands.

Perhaps like Juliet he could come alive
To hate Longfellow and to outrage life,
But dare not from his wretched rusty stone,
Landmark for girls developing in slums.

Here he is local color, another crank;
Pawnshops and whores and sour little bars
Accept him. Neither alarming nor prophetic,
He pleases like a wop or a jack-o-lantern.

Others up town forgive his nasty eyes
Because he was sick and had a mind to err;
But he was never dirty like Hawthorne,
But boyish with his spooks and funerals

And clammy virgins. What else were his codes
But diagrams of hideouts of the mind
Plugged up with corpses and expensive junk,
Prosopopoeia to keep himself at bay?

Think of him as a cicerone with data
False as a waxworks and that understood
Ask pitifully for pain. Or think that now
Four cities claim him as France recommended.

2

EMPORIUM

HE MUST have read Aladdin who rubbed his head
And brought this out of space; some genie came
With bolts of lawn and rugs of heavy red,
Shoes for white boxes, gems for velvet trays;
For who could authorize in his right name
Such pricelessness of time and recklessness of days?

Not Faust, who longed for Hell, would sell his light
For moving stairs and mirrors set in miles
Where wives might wander with their sex in sight;
Rage and rat's-logic this man must have known
Who built these buttresses on rotted piles,
Initialed every brick, and carved his lips in stone.

As if the ancient principle obtained
And solvent time would underwrite his debt,
Or the strong face of flesh were not profaned
For manikins with hair of cloth-of-gold;
As if no tongue had ever questioned yet
Who buys and who is bought, who sells and who is sold.

But those politely dressed in normal drab
Shall think of him remotely, think with shame
How of their skill, their goodness and their gab
He trained his joys to be obsequious Jews;
At last not even wives shall goad his name
To feats of wealth, humility, and sickness news;

So that, with rounded ruins honored, like Stonehenge,
Time shall have time, and he his impotent revenge.

UNIVERSITY

TO HURT the Negro and avoid the Jew
Is the curriculum. In mid-September
The entering boys, identified by hats,
Wander in a maze of mannered brick
    Where boxwood and magnolia brood
    And columns with imperious stance
    Like rows of ante-bellum girls
        Eye them, outlanders.

In whited cells, on lawns equipped for peace,
Under the arch, and lofty banister,
Equals shake hands, unequals blankly pass;
The exemplary weather whispers, 'Quiet, quiet'
    And visitors on tiptoe leave
    For the raw North, the unfinished West,
    As the young, detecting an advantage,
        Practice a face.

Where, on their separate hill, the colleges,
Like manor houses of an older law,
Gaze down embankments on a land in fee,
The Deans, dry spinsters over family plate,
    Ring out the English name like coin,
    Humor the snob and lure the lout.
    Within the precincts of this world
        Poise is a club.

But on the neighboring range, misty and high,
The past is absolute: some luckless race
Dull with inbreeding and conformity

Wears out its heart, and comes barefoot and bad
　　For charity or jail. The scholar
　　Sanctions their obsolete disease;
　　The gentleman revolts with shame
　　　　At his ancestor.

And the true nobleman, once a democrat,
Sleeps on his private mountain. He was one
Whose thought was shapely and whose dream was broad;
This school he held his art and epitaph.
　　But now it takes from him his name,
　　Falls open like a dishonest look,
　　And shows us, rotted and endowed,
　　　　Its senile pleasure.

WASHINGTON CATHEDRAL

FROM summer and the wheel-shaped city
That sweats like a swamp and wrangles on
Its melting streets, white mammoth Forums,
And political hotels with awnings, caryatids;
Past barricaded embassies with trees
That shed trash and parch his eyes,
To here, the acres of superior quiet,
Shadow and damp, the tourist comes,
And, cooled by stones and darkness, stares.

Tall as a lover's night, the nave
Broods over him, irradiates,
And stars of color out of painted glass
Shoot downward on apostles and on chairs
Huddled by hundred under altar rails.
Yet it is only Thursday; there are no prayers,

But exclamations. The lady invokes by name
The thousand-odd small sculptures, spooks,
New angels, pitted roods; she gives
The inventory of relics to his heart
That aches with history and astonishment:
He gives a large coin to a wooden coffer.

Outside, noon blazes in his face like guns.
He goes down by the Bishop's walk, the dial,
The expensive grass, the Byzantine bench,
While stark behind him a red naked crane
Hangs over the unfinished transept,
A Cubist hen rivalling the Gothic School.

Whether he sees the joke; whether he cares;
Whether he tempts a vulgar miracle,
Some deus ex machina, this is his choice,
A shrine of whispers and tricky penumbras.
    Therefore he votes again for the paid
Clergy, the English hint, the bones of Wilson
Crushed under tons of fake magnificence.
    Nor from the zoo of his instincts
    Come better than crude eagles: now
He cannot doubt that violent obelisk
And Lincoln whittled to a fool's colossus.
This church and city triumph in his eyes.
He is only a good alien, nominally happy.

ALEXANDRIA

THE thin Potomac scarcely moves
But to divide Virginia from today;
   Rider, whichever is your way
You go due south and neither South improves;
Not this, of fractured columns and queer rents
   And rags that charm the nationalist,
Not that, the axle of the continents,
Nor the thin sky that flows unprejudiced
This side and that, cleansing the poison breath.

For Thomas died a Georgian death
And now the legion bones of Arlington
   Laid out in marble alphabets
Stare on the great tombs of the capitol
   Where heroes calcified and cool
   Ponder the soldier named Unknown
Whose lips are guarded with live bayonets.

Yet he shall speak though sentries walk
And columns with their cold Corinthian stalk
   Shed gold-dust pollen on Brazil
   To turn the world to Roman chalk;
Yet he shall speak, yet he shall speak
   Whose sulphur lit the flood-lit Dome,
   Whose hands were never in the kill,
Whose will was furrows of Virginia loam.

But not like London blown apart by boys
Who learned the books of love in English schools,
His name shall strike the fluted columns down;

These shall lie buried deep as fifty Troys,
The money fade like leaves from green to brown,
And embassies dissolve to molecules.

/Then let the Negroes creep out of their scars
    And enter Alexandria
    To burn the clapboard and the straw
And cast a vote for whiteness and for trees.
The soldier now shall sit for Senators,
The whore for wives, the thief for justices.
    And have those others long to stay
When Roosevelt lunched on ballots yesterday
And Archibald performed the minuet?

THE SNOB

AT WHAT time in its little history
Did on the matrix of his brain a blow
Fall that struck like a relentless die
And left him speechless; or was it by degrees
That the algid folds of mind, caught in a pose,
       Hardened and set like concrete,
Printing and fixing a distorted moment?

Nothing but death will smash this ugly cast
That wears its trade mark big upon its face,
A scutcheon for Greek-letter brotherhoods
Where it is weakly sworn by smiles to cow
Unequals, niggers or just Methodists.
       His bearing is a school of thought,
But he is not funny and not unimportant.

THE GLUTTON

THE jowls of his belly crawl and swell like the sea
When his mandibles oily with lust champ and go wide;
Eternal, the springs of his spittle leak at the lips
Suspending the tongue like a whale that rolls on the tide.

His hands are as rotten fruit. His teeth are as corn.
Deep are the wells of his eyes and like navels, blind
Dough is the brain that supplies his passion with bread
Dough is the loose-slung sack of his great behind.

Will his paps become woman's? He dreams of the yielding
  of milk,
Despising the waste of his stool that recalls him to bread;
More than passion of sex and transverse pains of disease
He thinks of starvation, the locked-up mouth of the dead.

I am glad that his stomach will eat him away in revenge,
Digesting itself when his blubber is lain in the earth.
Let the juice of his gluttony swallow him inward like lime
And leave of his volume only the mould of his girth.

HOSPITAL

INSIDE or out, the key is pain. It holds
The florist to your pink medicinal rose,
The nickname to the corpse. One wipes it from
Blue German blades or drops it down the drain;
The novelist with a red tube up his nose
Gingerly pets it. Nurse can turn it off.

This is the Oxford of all sicknesses.
Kings have lain here and fabulous small Jews
And actresses whose legs were always news.
In this black room the painter lost his sight,
The crippled dancer here put down her shoes,
And the scholar's memory broke, like an old clock.

These reached to heaven and inclined their heads
While starchy angels reached them into beds:
These stooped to hell to labor out their time,
Or choked to death in seas of glaucous slime:
All tasted fire, and then, their hate annealed,
Ate sad ice-cream and wept upon a child.

What church is this, what factory of souls
Makes the bad good and fashions a new nose,
And the doctors reel with Latin and even the dead
Expect the unexpected? For O the souls
Fly back like heavy homing-birds to roost
In long-racked limbs, filling the lonely boughs.

The dead cry *life* and stagger up the hill;
But is there still the incorrigible city where
The well enjoy their poverty and the young

44

Worship the gutter? Is Wednesday still alive
And Tuesday wanting terribly to sin?
Hush, there are many pressing the oak doors,

Saying, "Are boys and girls important fears?
Can you predict the elections by my guts?"
But the rubber gloves are deep in a deep wound,
Stitching a single heart. These far surpass
Themselves, their wives, and the removed goitre;
Are, for the most part, human but unbandaged.

MONGOLIAN IDIOT

A D O G that spoke, a monster born of sheep
We mercilessly kill, and kill the thought,
Yet house the parrot and let the centaur go,
These being to their nature and those not.
We laugh at apes, that never quite succeed
        At eating soup or wearing hats.

Adam had named so many but not this,
This that would name a curse when it had come,
Unfinished man, or witch, or myth, or sin,
Not ever father and never quite a son.
Ape had outstripped him, dog and darling lamb
        And all the kindergarten beasts.

Enter the bare room of his mind and count
His store of words with letters large and black;
See how he handles clumsily those blocks
With swans and sums; his colored picture books.
At thirty-five he squeals to see the ball
        Bounce in the air and roll away.

Pity and fear we give this innocent
Who maimed his mother's beautiful instinct;
But she would say, "My body had a dog;
I bore the ape and nursed the crying sheep.
He is my kindness and my splendid gift
        Come from all life and for all life."

WAITRESS

WHOEVER with the compasses of his eyes
Is plotting the voyage of your steady shape
As you come laden through the room and back
And rounding your even bottom like a Cape
Crooks his first finger, whistles through his lip
Till you arrive, all motion, like a ship,

He is my friend—consider his dark pangs
And love of Niger, naked indigence,
Dance him the menu of a poem and squirm
Deep in the juke-box jungle, green and dense.
Surely he files his teeth, punctures his nose,
Carves out the god and takes off all his clothes.

For once, the token on the table's edge
Sufficing, proudly and with hair unpinned
You mounted the blueplate, stretched out and grinned
Like Christmas fish and turkey pink and skinned,
Eyes on the half-shell, loin with parsley stuck,
Thigh bones and ribs and little toes to suck.

I speak to you, ports of the northern myth,
This dame is carved and eaten. One by one,
God knows what hour, her different parts go home,
Lastly her pants, and day or night is done;
But on the restaurant the sign of fear
Reddens and blazes—"English spoken here."

MIDNIGHT SHOW

THE year is done, the last act of the vaudeville,
The last top hat and patent leather tappity-tap
Enclosed in darkness. Pat. Blackout. Only the organ
Groans, groans, its thousand golden throats in love;
While blue lowlight suffuses mysteries of sleep
Through racks of heads, and smoothly parts the gauzy vei
That slips, the last pretense of peace, into the wings.

With raucous crash the music rises to its feet,
And pouring from the hidden eye like God the Light
The light white-molten cold fills out the vacant field
With shattered cities, striped ships, and maps with lines
That crawl—symbols of horror, symbols of obscenity;
A girl astride a giant cannon, holding a flag;
Removal of stone and stained glass saints from a know
    cathedral.

And the Voice, the loving and faithful pointer, trots besi
Reel after reel, taking death in its well-trained stride.
The Voice, the polite, the auctioneer, places his hints
Like easy bids. The lab assistant, the Voice, dips
Their pity like litmus papers into His rancid heart.—
Dream to be surfeited, nerves clogged up with messages,
And, backed up at the ganglion, the news refused.

Dream to be out in snow where every corner Santa,
Heart of one generation's dreams, tinkles a bell.
We know him too. He is the Unemployed, but clowns
As the Giver, receiving pennies in a cast-iron pot.
Dream to be cold with Byrd at the world's bottom. Dream

To be warm in the Vatican, photographing a manuscript.
Dream to be there, a cell in Europe's poisoned blood.

Revulsion cannot rouse our heads for pride or protest.
The eye sees as the camera, a clean moronic gaze,
And to go is not impossible but merely careless.
O wife, what shall we tell the children that we saw?
O son, what shall we tell our father? And O my friend,
What shall we tell our senses when the lights go up
And noiselessly the golden curtains crash together!

HOLLYWOOD

FARTHEST from any war, unique in time
Like Athens or Baghdad, this city lies
Between dry purple mountains and the sea.
The air is clear and famous, every day
Bright as a postcard, bringing bungalows
     And sights. The broad nights advertise
For love and music and astronomy.

Heart of a continent, the hearts converge
On open boulevards where palms are nursed
With flare-pots like a grove, on villa roads
Where castles cultivated like a style
Breed fabulous metaphors in foreign stone,
     And on enormous movie lots
Where history repeats its vivid blunders.

Alice and Cinderella are most real.
Here may the tourist, quite sincere at last,
Rest from his dream of travels. All is new,
No ruins claim his awe, and permanence,
Despised like customs, fails at every turn.
     Here where the eccentric thrives,
Laughter and love are leading industries.

Luck is another. Here the body-guard,
The parasite, the scholar are well paid,
The quack erects his alabaster office,
The moron and the genius are enshrined,
And the mystic makes a fortune quietly;
     Here all superlatives come true
And beauty is marketed like a basic food.

O can we understand it? Is it ours,
A crude whim of a beginning people,
A private orgy in a secluded spot?
Or alien like the word *harem,* or true
Like hideous Pittsburgh or depraved Atlanta?
    Is adolescence just as vile
As this its architecture and its talk?

Or are they parvenus, like boys and girls?
Or ours and happy, cleverest of all?
Yes. Yes. Though glamorous to the ignorant
This is the simplest city, a new school.
What is more nearly ours? If soul can mean
    The civilization of the brain,
This is a soul, a possibly proud Florence.

AUTO WRECK

ITS quick soft silver bell beating, beating,
And down the dark one ruby flare
Pulsing out red light like an artery,
The ambulance at top speed floating down
Past beacons and illuminated clocks
Wings in a heavy curve, dips down,
And brakes speed, entering the crowd.
The doors leap open, emptying light;
Stretchers are laid out, the mangled lifted
And stowed into the little hospital.
Then the bell, breaking the hush, tolls once,
And the ambulance with its terrible cargo
Rocking, slightly rocking, moves away,
As the doors, an afterthought, are closed.

We are deranged, walking among the cops
Who sweep glass and are large and composed.
One is still making notes under the light.
One with a bucket douches ponds of blood
Into the street and gutter.
One hangs lanterns on the wrecks that cling,
Empty husks of locusts, to iron poles.

Our throats were tight as tourniquets,
Our feet were bound with splints, but now,
Like convalescents intimate and gauche,
We speak through sickly smiles and warn
With the stubborn saw of common sense,
The grim joke and the banal resolution.
The traffic moves around with care,

But we remain, touching a wound
That opens to our richest horror.
Already old, the question Who shall die?
Becomes unspoken Who is innocent?
For death in war is done by hands;
Suicide has cause and stillbirth, logic;
And cancer, simple as a flower, blooms.
But this invites the occult mind,
Cancels our physics with a sneer,
And spatters all we knew of denouement
Across the expedient and wicked stones.

HONKYTONK

TAKEN as diagram of Mind that marks,
Led by an arrow, green perimeters
Where thoughts sip peace and garden; inward then
To suffering junctions, slums kicked by a boot,
        Arpeggios of porches:
        Decision, Anger, Pride,
Like Self-Reproach the city points to this
Its maudlin slapping heart, our origin.

Then at the outskirts of our Conscious, No
From old high-over offices beats down
On standard faces Business-mad, and girls,
Grass under sullen stone, grown pale with work;
        Yet shields with shadow this
        Disgraced like genitals
Ghetto of local sin, laughable Hell,
Night's very alley, loathed but let alone.

I say to harass projects of decorum
This is maintained by kids, police, douceurs,
And ravenous for marvels, rancid Jews.
Callow as brass, their eyes on nipples snagged,
        Snagged in the jaded hair,
        Goaded by silken legs,
They mill around, bacterial and bright,
Seeking outbreaks of pain, their bitter milk.

Who needs Revenge or Fear can buy: in bars
Murals of lust, and talk; movies for men;
A waxworks of syphilitics; shooting range,

Phrenologist and tattoo artist; all
          Quacks who apprehend
          And speak the dirty word.
But oh, ridiculously lost those four
Hymning salvation at the Burlesk door.

How elemental ions of pure joy
Convert to deadly sins, and bump like trucks
Uptown to roads instinctive to the young,
I only ask. But in and out they go
          Satanic to discover
          Imago of Unrest
Whose Ultima Thule is a general low
And obscene civics of our self-distrust.

THE FLY

O HIDEOUS little bat, the size of snot,
With polyhedral eye and shabby clothes,
To populate the stinking cat you walk
The promontory of the dead man's nose,
Climb with the fine leg of a Duncan-Phyfe
    The smoking mountains of my food
        And in a comic mood
    In mid-air take to bed a wife.

Riding and riding with your filth of hair
On gluey foot or wing, forever coy,
Hot from the compost and green sweet decay,
Sounding your buzzer like an urchin toy—
You dot all whiteness with diminutive stool,
    In the tight belly of the dead
        Burrow with hungry head
    And inlay maggots like a jewel.

At your approach the great horse stomps and paws
Bringing the hurricane of his heavy tail;
Shod in disease you dare to kiss my hand
Which sweeps against you like an angry flail;
Still you return, return, trusting your wing
    To draw you from the hunter's reach
        That learns to kill to teach
    Disorder to the tinier thing.

My peace is your disaster. For your death
Children like spiders cup their pretty hands
And wives resort to chemistry of war.
In fens of sticky paper and quicksands

You glue yourself to death. Where you are stuck
   You struggle hideously and beg
      You amputate your leg
   Imbedded in the amber muck.

But I, a man, must swat you with my hate,
Slap you across the air and crush your flight,
Must mangle with my shoe and smear your blood,
Expose your little guts pasty and white,
Knock your head sidewise like a drunkard's hat,
   Pin your wings under like a crow's,
      Tear off your flimsy clothes
   And beat you as one beats a rat.

Then like Gargantua I stride among
The corpses strewn like raisins in the dust,
The broken bodies of the narrow dead
That catch the throat with fingers of disgust.
I sweep. One gyrates like a top and falls
   And stunned, stone blind, and deaf
      Buzzes its frightful F
   And dies between three cannibals.

TERMINAL

OVER us stands the broad electric face
With semaphores that flick into the gaps,
Notching the time on sixtieths of space,
Springing the traveller through the folded traps
Downstairs with luggage anywhere to go
While others happily toil upward too;
Well-dressed or stricken, banished or restored,
Hundreds step down and thousands get aboard.

In neat confusion, tickets in our brain
We press the hard plush to our backs and sigh;
The brakeman thumbs his watch, the children strain
The windows to their smeary sight—Goodbye,
The great car creaks, the stone wall turns away
And lights flear past like fishes undersea;
Heads rolling heavily and all as one
With languid screams we charge into the sun.

Now through the maelstrom of the town we ride
Clicking with speed like skates on solid ice;
Streets drop and buildings silently collide,
Rails spread apart, converge and neatly splice.
Through gasping blanks of air we pound and ford
Bulking our courage forward like a road,
Climbing the world on long dead-level stairs
With catwalk stilts and trestles hung by hairs.

Out where the oaks on wide turntables grow
And constellation hamlets gyre and glow,
The straight-up bridges dive and from below
The river's sweet eccentric borders flow;

Into the culverts sliced like lands of meat,
Armies of cornstalks on their ragged feet,
And upward-outward toward the blueback hill
Where clouds of thunder graze and drink their fill.

And always at our side, swifter than we
The racing rabbits of the wire lope
And in their blood the words at liberty
Outspeed themselves; but on our rail we grope
Drinking from one white wire overhead
Hot drinks of action and hell's fiery feed.
Lightly the finger-shaped antennae feel
And lightly cheer the madness of our wheel.

We turn, we turn, thrumming the harp of sounds
And all is pleasure's move, motion of joy;
Now we imagine that we go like hounds
And now like sleds and now like many a toy
Coming alive on Christmas Day to crawl
Between the great world of the floor and wall,
But on the peak of speed we flag and fall—
Fixed on the air we do not move at all.

Arrived at space we settle in our car
And stare like souls admitted to the sky;
Nothing at length is close at hand or far;
All feats of image vanish from the eye.
Upon our brow is set the bursting star,
Upon the void the wheel and axle-bar,
The planetary fragments broken lie;
Distance is dead and light can only die.

DRUG STORE

I do remember an apothecary,
And hereabouts 'a dwells

IT BAFFLES the foreigner like an idiom,
And he is right to adopt it as a form
Less serious than the living-room or bar;
      For it disestablishes the cafe,
Is a collective, and on basic country.

Not that it praises hygiene and corrupts
The ice-cream parlor and the tobacconist's
Is it a center; but that the attractive symbols
      Watch over puberty and leer
Like rubber bottles waiting for sick-use.

Youth comes to jingle nickels and crack wise;
The baseball scores are his, the magazines
Devoted to lust, the jazz, the coca-cola,
      The lending-library of love's latest.
He is the customer; he is heroized.

And every nook and cranny of the flesh
Is spoken to by packages with wiles.
'Buy me, buy me,' they whimper and cajole;
      The hectic range of lipsticks pouts,
Revealing the wicked and the simple mouth.

With scarcely any evasion in their eye
They smoke, undress their girls, exact a stance;
But only for a moment. The clock goes round;
      Crude fellowships are made and lost;
They slump in booths like rags, not even drunk.

3

THE CONTRABAND

I DREAMED I held a poem and knew
The capture of a living thing.
Boys in a Grecian circle sang
And women at their harvesting.

Slowly I tried to wake and draw
The vision after, word by word,
But sleep was covetous: the song
The singers and the singing blurred.

The paper flowers of everynight
All die. Day has no counterpart,
Where memory writes its boldface wish
And swiftly punishes the heart.

NOSTALGIA

MY SOUL stands at the window of my room,
    And I ten thousand miles away;
My days are filled with Ocean's sound of doom,
    Salt and cloud and the bitter spray.
Let the wind blow, for many a man shall die.

My selfish youth, my books with gilded edge,
    Knowledge and all gaze down the street;
The potted plants upon the window ledge
    Gaze down with selfish lives and sweet.
Let the wind blow, for many a man shall die.

My night is now her day, my day her night,
    So I lie down, and so I rise;
The sun burns close, the star is losing height,
    The clock is hunted down the skies.
Let the wind blow, for many a man shall die.

Truly a pin can make the memory bleed,
    A world explode the inward mind
And turn the skulls and flowers never freed
    Into the air, no longer blind.
Let the wind blow, for many a man shall die.

Laughter and grief join hands. Always the heart
    Clumps in the breast with heavy stride;
The face grows lined and wrinkled like a chart,
    The eyes bloodshot with tears and tide.
Let the wind blow, for many a man shall die.
            (March 19, 1942. Indian Ocean)

A CUT FLOWER

I STAND on slenderness all fresh and fair,
I feel root-firmness in the earth far down,
I catch in the wind and loose my scent for bees
That sack my throat for kisses and suck love.
What is the wind that brings thy body over?
Wind, I am beautiful and sick. I long
For rain that strikes and bites like cold and hurts.
Be angry, rain, for dew is kind to men
When I am cool from sleep and take my bath.

Who softens the sweet earth about my feet?
Touches my face so often and brings water?
Where does she go, taller than any sunflower
Over the grass like birds? Has she a root?
These are great animals that kneel to us,
Sent by the sun perhaps to help us grow.
I have seen death. The colors went away,
The petals grasped at nothing and curled tight.
Then the whole head fell off and left the sky.

She tended me and held me by my stalk.
Yesterday I was well, and then the gleam,
The thing sharper than frost cut me in half.
I fainted and was lifted high. I feel
Waist-deep in rain. My face is dry and drawn.
My beauty leaks into the glass like rain.
When first I opened to the sun I thought
My colors would be parched. Where are my bees?
Must I die now? Is this a part of life?

(July 20, 1942. Australia)

BARTER

CHANGE flesh with me, old man;
Lend me your sagging face
For a laughing even tan
And a wrist alive as a race;
Lend me a silver beard
Or a mumbling chin
For a head sharp-eyed, sharp-eared
And a jaw that's thin.
Old man, old man, old man,
Will you give up your loins
For the crazy hips of a boy
And a trunk that joins
To a woman's joy?
Will you part with your fears and aches,
The grave in your dream,
The knee that buckles and quakes,
The brown blood's sluggish stream?
Will you? Will you? Will you
Lend me your body a year,
The year age comes to kill you?
Will you let me hear and peer
From your face for a day,
To touch with your touch, fear with your fear,
And hear your name my name
And say your final famous say
That famous final fatal day?

SELF-HISTORY

THE times and phases of self-history
Are stratified and buried like layers of
Antique cities solid in one mound.

In which little area of being
I have erected and seen fall empires of hope,
Seen towers crack and white walls break like waves!

Growth was earth-tremors
Volcanic fire
Famine
And the slow siege of war.

Who can no longer build under the sun
I hourly go down among the litter
The stony lava
And the bones,

Sole digger in these pits,
Hunting
With the terrible pity of owner and poet
For the shattered god-face
And the once-cool shrine.

PARADOX: THE BIRDS

WRONG about birds. I cannot call
That swift, enslaved, mechanical
Come and go, come and go,
Build and feed and mate and grow
      Beautiful.
Beautiful, the poets are wrong
To love you for your turn and wheel and glide and song

Beast of the wind, wolf of the tree,
Heart with the gunner's history,
Rise and fall, rise and fall,
Heart of the heart I cannot call
      Liberty.
Liberty, the poets are wrong
To love you for your turn and wheel and glide and song

HAIRCUT

O WONDERFUL nonsense of lotions of Lucky Tiger,
Of savory soaps and oils of bottle-bright green,
The gold of liquers, the unguents of Newark and Niger,
Powders and balms and waters washing me clean,

In mirrors of marble and silver I see us forever
Increasing, decreasing the puzzles of luminous spaces
As I turn, am revolved and pumped in the air on a lever,
With the backs of my heads in chorus with all of my faces.

Scissors and comb are mowing my hair into neatness,
Now pruning my ears, now smoothing my neck like a plain;
In the harvest of hair and the chaff of powdery sweetness
My snow-covered slopes grow dark with the wooly rain.

And the little boy cries, for it hurts to sever the curl,
And we too are quietly bleating to part with our coat.
Does the barber want blood in a dish? I am weak as a girl,
I desire my pendants, the fatherly chin of a goat.

I desire the pants of a bear, the nap of a monkey
Which trousers of friction have blighted down to my skin.
I am bare as a tusk, as jacketed up as a flunkey,
With the chest of a moth-eaten camel growing within.

But in death we shall flourish, you summer-dark leaves of
    my head.
While the flesh of the jaw ebbs away from the shores of
    my teeth;
You shall cover my sockets and soften the boards of my bed
And lie on the flat of my temples as proud as a wreath.

HOW LONG AGO THE HOME

H O W long ago the home
The custody of womb
How far far out of mind
In another dimension
The aberration
Of first information,
Goodbye to it, it must have been unkind.

Sister I teased you
Cousin I kissed you
Hid in the closet
In female odors
Above the disorders
Of grandfather's illness.
The confusing passion
For guilty action
The search for sadness
In the other's stillness
Were these but profits
Of an instant mood
Or the lust for pity
In the rising blood?

ELEGY WRITTEN
ON A FRONTPORCH

THE sun burns on its sultry wick;
Stratus and cumulus unite.
I who am neither well nor sick
Sit in a wicker chair and write.

A hot wind presses at my lips.
I peel. Am totally undressed.
Pinkish, as through a part-eclipse,
Heat licks upon my naked breast.

Angles in quick succession rise.
Eyesight is stereopticon
As roof and roof geometrize
Perspective deviously drawn.

I face a heaven half-destroyed,
A skyscape alabaster, dead.
One living shadow on the void,
A Flying Fortress drones ahead.

Motion and fixity take shape;
The fallow rays intensify
Distinctness. Nothing can escape
The clean hard focus of the eye.

Noise into humming noise constricts;
The traffic mumbles deeper down.
Only a trolley contradicts,
Ticks by neurotically to town.

Stretched taut upon the light I scorch,
Writhe in my sweat and smoke and sun.
The evening paper hits the porch;
My honeymoon of peace is done.

Unmasticated pulp of life . . .
Decision finds me blind and deaf.
I do not finger for the strife
Of Delano and Mutt and Jeff,

Or bend upon my nudity's
Umbilicus, the fact of facts,
As one who drowns in light and sees
The newsreel of his private acts.

I do not hug my feet with glee
And smile into my cul-de-sac
Enamoured of the dignity
Of facing forward moving back.

But set my wired sight, reclaim
The rotted friendship and the fresh;
Tune in on him who changed his name
And her who stultified the flesh.

I see who came to marriage raw
With poverty and self-abuse;
Defendants to the general law,
Their ignorance was no excuse.

Instructors, graduates I see,
Scholars who sneered into their books,
The female doctors pouring tea,
Hundreds of victims of their looks.

The money-poise of some, the pride
Of those who whored on easy checks,

Sons of The Business, dressy, snide,
Disfigured in expensive wrecks.

Believers in the songhit, thin
With pounding to the hebroid jazz;
The studious drinkers feeding in
The cloaca of the middle-class.

I see too many who romanced
Defeat, unmasculine, debased;
The striptease puritans who danced
The long lewd ritual of waste.

All these I bury out of sight
Sans benefit of epitaph.
I turn my legs into the light,
Punch out a cigaret and laugh.

For one, the best against that rout,
Deserted, obdurate to see
Their weakly literate wear out
The old Horatian fallacy;

Spoke of the beauty-to-obey,
The life-expectancy of bone.
She turned her back upon the day
But will not lie at night alone.

TO EVELYN FOR CHRISTMAS

GREETING the hostile parents, you or I,
With sheepish bravery like the young who know
The exact extent of every household law—
But who are man and woman, soldier and wife,

Let us again today steal to our chair
And touch like rightful people in the house
Our bodies and our deep or trivial news
And the small fortune of our startled joy.

For your great heart comes over me like sound
Of Christmas and your look and your bright arms
Balanced with packages and wreaths throw down
A heap of tokens for the world's birthday.

For Anno Domini, for the year of War
Hardness I give, a drop of medicine,
A tear to take which on your tender tongue
May be the poison or the dram of strength

To succour destiny or to destroy
The daily Christian you which is a fir
Warming the room with odours of surprise
And hung with points of light and boughs of green.

ODE FOR CLENCHED TEETH

THE absurdity of being better.
The terrible lure of being more.
See the days crowded with the print of years
Spinning like bookleaves in the wind.
When we think,
These are our days
Lying with the wind.

Of untold cold surging.
Precision planets blue as steel.
Of singing.
Of racing rocking through the void.
Of plunging the senseless orbit of a billion years.

And yet however nevertheless still otherwise
Discounting counting time
Time in our time
Like a toy train in a real ship sinking,
Time like a toy marked Made in Germany
Jiggling on a tin toy track
On a real table of a real cabin of a real ship
Sinking.

No wonder we listen.
Let the leaves sick of inaudible sounds listen.
Let the leaves wither in the silent poisonous noise,
Curling over the dried veins
Like a yellowed photograph of smashed Flanders.

DRUID HILL PARK

TO EIGHTY spurious summers of belief
    In itself, which was the stunted gift
And great green concept of a century;
    Wherever else it spread its aims
Of mournful groves and congeries of birds,
Gardens done lovingly, but also false;
To such pride and the then visible future,
    Confused, I dedicate these words.

When they had set the brook to wander,
    The pretty path for love's disaster
And the Moorish summer house given a role,
    Glad that the Mall was French but English,
The misty purlieus secretly defined,
    One day the bleeding flag stood over,
    The wind soughed, the city gathered,
And the mayor, the mayor, pronounced it beautiful.

(To the false pretences of its founders.)
Down in the inorganic streets a posse
Of sturdy grandpas were still maiming trees
Which fell repeatedly betrayed, like Indians,
And under the bell-glass on the mantel piece
    Our aunty's eyes were immortelles;
Likewise, before the park the band began,
The ribbon snapped, the carriages moved in.

Thereafter all was obsolete, in ruins,
And a name; to their pedantic masonry
    Moss was affixed and iron wreaths
And autumn's beautiful disease of bronze.

Sunday pressed pansies in a book,
Wednesday had a good cry, and on the lawn
In a slight drizzle the statue was unveiled,
Hooded and cold, to the inverted womb.

To come down to today: clubs for the rich,
Beaches and shows for us, and for the poor
    This vast ambiguous legacy,
No arboretum but an antique cirque,
    Mixed past and future, on which they build
    Their shanty and perfunctory present.
In this connection the benches, the hothouse,
    The beetle traps, the inferior zoo.

Decidedly they failed it who believed
    That beauty was female and foreign,
    Undressed unwholesome thoughts, or lockets.
From town they carried up like sacrifice
Their dirty minds and linen, nothing loath
    To scar with mosques the simplest hill,
    Or foul the air with poems whose finger
Led to the lip of graves their weeping wives.

II

Be good and with me walk
The old devalued park
Where autumn has set in
The sad colors run
And a foolish East built on
The very simplest of hills
Leads us away from work
And drinks our laughter through its walls

77

Nor need we laugh who have
An anger fit to live
Something to build upon
That from our conscious warm
Developed like a pun
Knows what to see and hurt
But never really raved
Being book bred to lie apart

Our Moorish no one asks
For mother's easy risks
Not here the lovers sin
To modify their ban
Some knowledge leaking in
Has rusted the roof like rain
And the whisper in the mosque
Is gone with hearts of the common run

Earth just as sweetly rots
Digesting its own fruits
Torpor adjusts to roots
And cannas set in hearts
Are lifted from their beds
O falls like winged seeds
The cry of living things
Upon whose house their death prevails

With you to apprehend
All seasons left behind
I am as child who hears
And loves what best he knows
Show me disease of bronze
Say it shall be gone
The poison in the wind
Removed leaving the wind alone

78

But for a just return
Take over hills we scorn
From years of private waste
Decades of trial and caste
Harvest our true response
To everything that grieves
To the cold light that burns
This brilliant dynasty of leaves

And give to sober sight
Now life removes his hat
Exactitude of aim
Not heavily to dream
Take all their fictions down
Like summer overthrown
Laugh in their face, show fight
Darling tell what it is to own

How lands declined like this
Abandoned piece by piece
And tax-free beautiful
Better than armies fell
O colder is just as well
We shall not hear them say
Here nature broke her lease
Here many another lover lay

SIX RELIGIOUS LYRICS

1

I SING the simplest flower,
    The earliest quest of day,
That wears in its white corrolla
    The signet of breathing May.

For the envelope of beauty
    Discloses the female part,
The bending and swollen stigma,
    The sly tongue of the heart.

And the dusty bee for nectar
    Enters and drinks his fill,
And the wind comes freely, freshly
    To assist the season's will.

I give you the simplest flower,
    The color of air, a dress
Self-woven and frail and holy,
    The signet of love's distress.

2

Upstairs the shuttles of the loom
Ravel and weave the shadow-play;
Downstairs on endless steps of gloom
Those souls in sorrowful array . . .

Gentlest decline of inward hills
That distance lightens and makes fair,
Valley of instruments that fills
The sibylline nocturnal air!

What innuendo of their cry
Will enter life and course the blood,
That gods and goddesses so high
May represent our earthly good?

What human kiss can take the place
Of these of such gigantic scope;
What joy describe the human face
Washed down the street in floods of hope?

3

Dark words, birds of the race
    That voyage time and birth
To pierce the columns of the East,
    Fossils of prayer and earth:

Grave words, words of the name
    That live from face to face,
Remembering love's antiquity,
    Exile and dead disgrace;

Iron words, oaths of the war,
    Seed of the seed of Cain,
Under whose mail and metal dew
    Our thousand youths are lain;

Is Babel there, fallen of heart,
    Unfinished on the sky,
Can speech renew the tribe of joy
    And Jesus justify?

4

The soldier's death occasions
   Seldom a bitter cry:
We feel in his abrasions
   A death that we deny.

To fall as such another
   And hundreds far and near
Is true for friend and brother,
   But false for us who fear.

Luck has a wider cover
   That Justice's or God's;
Our chances scarcely hover,
   The Exception sees and nods.

Saluting the death of any
   The mass will seldom grieve,
For out of the fall of many
   The one will rise and leave.

5

Treasure your anonymity,
You who remain, however torn,
Eldest of us and best of us,
Die silent and be silent born.

At length the elected must subside,
The honorable and the traitor kind,
And armies all repose in clay,
Corpses and booty left behind.

Inviolable and sacred mass,
You were not good but good enough,

You nodded at your destinies,
The last and next-to-last rebuff.

Nation and race and family
Have built on many a smoking town;
Samson was also slightly blind
But brought the roof of Dagon down.

6

for L. Q.

Witty of heart and pure of heart,
  In churches cavernous and dim
You drank the cup of Christ apart
  And knelt and worshipped Him.

Somewhere I waited for your arm
  And walked the traffic of broad day
Sadly, for all the earthly harm
  From which you turned to pray.

In cloisters where your sisters dwelled
  You walked in peace and dreamed to die;
You did not take the veil they held,
  The kiss to sanctify,

But pleasantly amongst us all
  Who doubt and shout and depredate
Live by the charity of Paul
  And keep the silent gate.

A ROBBERY

BY DAY I had dispraised their life,
Accused foremost the little cheated wives
Whose hands like trailers ludicrously hitched
To husbands, over the graph of business bump.
As often, with my friend, I laughed at them,
All but their young, whose strenuous anarchy
      Asked Why and promised war.

So of their legal dark of nights,
And bed revenge, and competent small births
That shut us out from marriage, I despaired:
Men brought home hate like evening papers, maids
Longed for their slums, the inarticulate clock
Spoke once, and faces, double-locked and still,
      Turned to the wall to sleep.

I show that fear unearthed that Boy.
Into the taut membrane of night, like knives
A woman screams, rending with rape our rest.
Bodies are ripped from beds; the snapped dream hangs:
And quick to plunge the torn portieres of sleep
We race soft-running Horror the length of halls.
      Ghouls are at every door.

Down in the hostile dark, as one,
The heavy faces point, close in, take aim,
And hands describe centripetal broad Wheels
Through which unseen a wiry robber moves.
Voices enlarge, cops clamber from the sky,
Our sudden symmetry dissolves. We laugh.
      "Nothing is caught, or lost."

Yet our emergency is lost,
Which would have, naked in the domestic night,
Brought us like actual murder to relief.
Boys have mixed blood and kissed to seal an oath.
Boys have an oath. O we were close to boys,
The salesman, the real estator, the clerk, and I,
      Their enemy, their poet.

Robber, paid agent of our hate,
I kiss my hand to you across the roofs
And jungle of back alleys where you hide.
You with your guns are like a boy I loved.
He was born dead and never had a name.
He was my little son. Night took him off.
      Hard to unlearn is love.

POET

Il arrive que l'esprit demande la poesie

LEFT leg flung out, head cocked to the right,
Tweed coat or army uniform, with book,
Beautiful eyes, who is this walking down?
Who, glancing at the pane of glass looks sharp
And thinks it is not he—as when a poet
Comes swiftly on some half-forgotten poem
And loosely holds the page, steady of mind,
        Thinking it is not his?

And when will *you* exist?—Oh, it is I,
Incredibly skinny, stooped, and neat as pie,
Ignorant as dirt, erotic as an ape,
Dreamy as puberty—with dirty hair!
Into the room like kangaroo he bounds,
Ears flopping like the most expensive hound's;
His chin received all questions as he bows
        Mouthing a green bon-bon.

Has no more memory than rubber. Stands
Waist-deep in heavy mud of thought and broods
At his own wetness. When he would get out,
To his surprise he lifts in air a phrase
As whole and clean and silvery as a fish.
Which jumps and dangles on his damned hooked grin,
But like a name-card on a man's lapel
        Calls him a conscious fool.

And childlike he remembers all his life
And cannily constructs it, fact by fact,

As boys paste postage stamps in careful books,
Denoting pence and legends and profiles,
Nothing more valuable.—And like a thief,
His eyes glassed over and concealed with guilt,
Fondles his secrets like a case of tools,
      And waits in empty doors.

By men despised for knowing what he is,
And by himself. But he exists for women.
As dolls to girls, as perfect wives to men,
So he to women. And to himself a thing,
All ages, epicene, without a trade.
To girls and wives always alive and fated;
To men and scholars always dead like Greek
      And always mistranslated.

Towards exile and towards shame he lures himself,
Tongue winding on his arm, and thinks like Eve
By biting apple will become most wise.
Sentio ergo sum: he feels his way
And words themselves stand up for him like Braille
And punch and perforate his parchment ear.
All language falls like Chinese on his soul,
      Image of song unsounded.

This is the coward's coward that in his dreams
Sees shapes of pain grow tall. Awake at night
He peers at sounds and stumbles at a breeze.
And none holds life less dear. For as a youth
Who by some accident observes his love
Naked and in some natural ugly act,
He turns with loathing and with flaming hands,
      Seared and betrayed by sight.

He is the business man, on beauty trades,
Dealer in arts and thoughts who, like the Jew,

Shall rise from slums and hated dialects
A tower of bitterness. Shall be always strange,
Hunted and then sought after. Shall be sat
Like an ambassador from another race
At tables rich with music. He shall eat flowers,
Chew honey and spit out gall. They shall all smile
          And love and pity him.

His death shall be by drowning. In that hour
When the last bubble of pure heaven's air
Hovers within his throat, safe on his bed,
A small eternal figurehead in terror,
He shall cry out and clutch his days of straw
Before the blackest wave. Lastly, his tomb
Shall list and founder in the troughs of grass.
          And none shall speak his name.